MIDNIGHT IN A PERFECT WORLD

MIDNIGHT IN A PERFECT WORLD

POEMS

COLLIN KELLEY

SIBLING RIVALRY PRESS
LITTLE ROCK / ARKANSAS | DISTURB / ENRAPTURE

Midnight in a Perfect World
Copyright © 2018 by Collin Kelley
Author photo by Colin Potts
Cover design by Seth Pennington

All rights reserved. No part of this book may be reproduced or republished without written consent from the publisher, except by reviewers who may quote brief excerpts in connection with a review in a newspaper, magazine, or electronic publication; nor may any part of this book be reproduced, stored in a retrieval system, or transmitted in any form, or by any means be recorded without written consent of the publisher.

Sibling Rivalry Press, LLC
PO Box 26147
Little Rock, AR 72221
info@siblingrivalrypress.com
www.siblingrivalrypress.com

ISBN: 978-1-943977-53-6
Library of Congress Control No. 2018941800

This title is housed permanently in the Rare Books and Special Collections Vault of the Library of Congress.

First Sibling Rivalry Press Edition, November 2018

For Christopher Jason Siddons

1
THE URGE FOR GOING

15	Feast
16	Night Ride Home
17	Bitch
19	20th Century Boy
20	Nineteen
21	Strange Weather
22	Killing Time
23	Revenant
25	Kate Bush Appears on Night Flight, 1981
26	I Should Be So Lucky
28	The panic of wanting you
29	Ghost Dancing
30	What I'm Wearing
32	Things to do in Denver when you'd rather be dead
34	Another Monica Bellucci Dream
36	The unrequited arsonist

2
THIS IS NOT AMERICA

39	Incantation
40	In Tavistock Square
41	Room 335, Royal National Hotel
42	Rochester Station
43	Dukker
44	In the cut
46	Nostalgia
47	The comedown
48	Victoria Gate
49	Atonement
51	The Voyage In
53	The Turf
54	English pastoral
55	Ritual
56	In the afterlife my father is a London cab driver
57	Midnight in a Perfect World

Insight, foresight, more sight—
the clock on the wall reads a quarter past midnight.

~ DJ Shadow / Organized Konfusion
"Midnight in a Perfect World"

PART ONE
THE URGE FOR GOING

FEAST

All the poems will be about you,
so stop asking.
But I won't write them here.
I'll take to the sky, other continents,
count the blessings of learning
to pack lightly, to make room.
John Irving said sorrow floats,
but it also flies and I've tucked it
between clean socks and underwear,
shaken it out in unfamiliar rooms.
I'm going to write about you
and all the others who insinuated
themselves into my life and thought
they could get away scot-free.
I'm going to name names,
take back my own, be self-indulgent.
Those New England confessionals
will have nothing on me.
I will come home,
my bags bulging from the purge,
and I will read it to everyone.
This will be a slaughter,
followed by a field dressing,
but there will be no trip to the butcher.
Your head won't become a trophy.
I'm going to bring you home,
sit in the dark and eat you raw
all over again.

NIGHT RIDE HOME

Tonight, on the way home from teaching a poetry workshop, the wind tries to take my car, buffets the windows, steers me to the right. The sky opens its mouth and issues clouds that glow toxic red over the city, and Joni Mitchell is on the radio singing a song I first heard in college: *What do I do here with this hunger...*

There were eight eager faces shining at me like moons, and I had all my favorite poets tucked under my arm—some dead, some alive, and me somewhere in between. I guessed that the girl wearing a pink sweater was from Sussex, England just by her accent, and the shock and pleasure on her face gave me a Henry Higgins-esque thrill. I let her talk too much, just to hear her voice. After class, the professor said it was the most he'd heard the girl say all semester.

Maybe it's the books sliding around on the seat, or maybe it's those magazines that came in the mail reminding me I haven't seen London in two years. Anything seems possible on nights like this, as I drive steady into the wind, mentally emptying my bank account, devising an escape plan, wondering who will recognize my accent when I am far from home, reading poetry, more alive than dead.

BITCH

Bitch, you are sleeping with my man,
are the first words I hear
when I answer the phone.

Bitch, I want some answers from you,
he screams, as if it's my fault,
like I held a gun to his man's head,
forced his lean frame to settle
into my soft folds every Friday.

Bitch, I want to know how you met him.
As if this matters now, but it was an app,
an agreement for anonymous sex.
Who knew it would be so good, who knew
it would become habit, that it might evolve?

Bitch, what is he to you?
Good question, because the last time
Randal's kisses were hungrier,
his small talk heavier, subtly changing
the rules of engagement.
We'd been on this brink for ages,
the fall from sex into love.

Bitch, you fucking bitch.
I accept this condemnation, the anger,
all those years of fidelity up in smoke.
But I couldn't resist, intoxicated by the scent

of Djarums in his dreadlocks that shrouded
like a wedding veil as he moved above me.
For two years he's been calling my name,
and I don't even know yours.

20TH CENTURY BOY
— for Ken

The night I screamed you out of my life
for good, I fed your confettied photo
to swirling toilet—a ticker tape parade
and dead fish burial rolled into one.

Later, I found the box, a jiffy popped
trove of forgotten snapshots. You
bursting in full color from every slick
surface: sulky, smirky, your mouth
issuing smoke, cigarette blurred
in your expressive hands.

If I hold them just right, I can make
a flip book of that last day,
bring you back to animated life.
The shots where you're walking away
snapping through my fingers,
your back retreating in increments.
And if I flip the other way,
you coming back.

NINETEEN

Up for anything pliable
nothing out of bounds
dress you up dress you down
undress you in public

Far from home no witnesses
this is space exploration
boundary breaking
daddy's long arm can't reach you here

Sidewalk swagger dissolves
to breathless whisper begging
for release for tongues
your mouth a light socket

STRANGE WEATHER

And he's the rain that they predicted, it's the forecast every time.
— Marianne Faithfull

You almost convinced me that you weren't beautiful. My memory at odds with your poorly lit selfies, claims of weight gain, acne, restless legs. We had one cinematic brief encounter, followed by tearful farewells in a perfect rain. Eight months later, we meet again on the tail end of a lightning storm. Watching your approach from the hotel lobby window—tailored black coat, not a hair out of place, taller than I remembered—I see people on the street stare, one over his shoulder, and I know that this second meeting will be a mistake.

You sidestep a public embrace, draw back uncertainly in the elevator, catch your reflection in the mirror. Maybe, for the first time, realize just how beautiful you are. Then we are alone in the room, naked on the bed. At least your kisses seem realistic, hungry from distance, but then we both say I love you, which is a lie, but part of the game as you pin and enter me, your fingers interlacing with mine as I bury my head in the pillow to spare the guests next door of my empty pleasure. This long-distance fantasy should have been left to midnight calls, pinging texts, our cries and whispers bouncing off towers and satellite relays, up in the clouds where our heads have been.

Later, I await the message that you're home safely, but it never comes. It's raining again in Manhattan, a lone rumble of thunder like a bell tolling underwater, and I find myself in that odd purgatory of mourning something that never was.

KILLING TIME

I can almost pretend I'm elsewhere.
Half past four, the light nearly gone,
like that afternoon walk in Leicester Square
when I was filled with dark joy.
The cold and damp bone deep
in that pervasive London way.

I grew up in an oppressive climate,
air leaden with hiss and moisture.
I envy regions with short days,
charting weather patterns
for low-lying clouds and threats of rain.
My cure for seasonal affective disorder—
turn out the lights.

Autumn comes later now,
thanks to politicians and lobbyists
with nothing better to do than kill time.
Day lingers as landscapes turn grey,
the wind in the leaves telegraphing
in cracks and shudders
for the night to come.

REVENANT
— for Peter

One-upmanship over dive bar beer and burgers,
cigarette smoke curling toward scorched ceiling.
We're seat fillers, interchangeable souls going to ash,
tears and queers a dime a dozen here—
can't tell one from the other without a program.

We had sex last night, not with each other,
but we might as well have. It would save us
the trouble of totting up the score,
our extravagant, unquenchable appetites.
I've never been so fat and so empty, I think,
while you casually mention falling off the wagon.
And why not? You're 32 and single again.

It's been a decade since we said goodbye,
when I left you levitating on the floor
in the wake of mushrooms and silver spoons,
and I could take stairs without losing my breath.
When I thought I'd never have sex again
without your face floating above me,
disembodied, superimposed, like smoke
filling my pores and follicles.

Today when I put on my coat,
I caught the scent of last night, of you,
of what cannot ever truly be aired out.
Love does not remain, but every now and then

a random man will touch me
in just the right spot, whisper his desires,
and you will surface, a revenant
impervious to exorcism,
even when I call some other's name.

KATE BUSH APPEARS ON NIGHT FLIGHT, 1981

Midnight in the forbidden living room, closing doors quietly behind me, unknowingly opening a path from which I will never veer, even later when I become older, succumbing to any zeitgeist.

I turn on the TV and she somersaults across the screen, startling the rolling vertical hold into stillness, her siren voice makes me fumble in the dark for volume control. I put my hand against the screen, feel the static in my fingertips, a transference of energy in 1981 that delineates past and present. A woman who calls herself Cathy wants to come in through the window.

But she wasn't coming through, I was going in, my link to her a series of hot boxes where she would appear without warning over decades like the Virgin, her songs a catechism, her name a prayer I chanted at the backs of retreating lovers, divorcing parents and death, and even in her absence, the music never faltered like I did, songs willing pills back into bottles.

That night I put on my armor, never had a ring put on my finger, blew kisses across the ocean, for inspiration and strength, for God to keep her even when he wasn't keeping me, and now, when I am driving or dancing, walking in Los Angeles or London, the song remains the same, her name an utterance: *Kate, Kate, Kate*.

I SHOULD BE SO LUCKY

Kylie Minogue is working the drive-thru
at some fast food joint in Middle England.
It rises out of a green pasture, solitary,
a beckoning trans-fat Stonehenge.

Having mastered driving on the left,
I roll up to the window,
which opens like a vacuum sealed bag,
and the tiny pop princess smiles,
pink lips pull back over perfect teeth,
her hair pinned under a paper cap,
name emblazoned on a shit-brown uniform,
hand-jiving to "The Loco-motion,"
asks if I want fish and chips.

The music changes suddenly, turns
high-pitched, like tinnitus or tuning fork,
resonating at time-altering frequency.
Just when I think my head might explode,
the world goes white and quiet.
Kylie reaches through the window,
shows me her palm, and tattooed there is 1988.
Because it's only make-believe, she sings,
then hands me a greasy bag.

When I open it, I can see myself inside with Clint,
sitting in our high school classroom 20 years ago,
desire as strong as the fetid oil and fat

that heat-shimmers from the sack.
And when I close it, written on the outside
in the creases and stains are the words
live or die.

THE PANIC OF WANTING YOU

comes unexpectedly, distant need
close now, roaring in my ears,
how quickly it becomes irrational.

Where are you? Where have you been?
Where are you going?
How did you survive before the day we met?

Waiting for your call, the throb of it
in my hand, signal always on,
always transmitting.

How suddenly I am in the wrong house,
my rationale pounding on the door,
picking locks, testing windows

for any entry, because even as I
temporarily lose control, both of us—
my two halves—know it's nothing more

than misplaced desire.
This is New Orleans, after all.
It comes with the rain.

GHOST DANCING

Here are my eyes, highlighted like film noir
through cracked window blinds.
Streetlights wink off plunging the parking lot
into creeping shadows, only to be revealed
in brief moonlight as trash cans, waving branches,
a homeless man pissing beside a car.

And my rooms are pitcher than pitch:
dried blood brick walls, painted concrete floor,
low ceiling swallowing furniture.
The only pinpoint of light the peephole,
glowing like some distant galaxy on the other side
of the room, or maybe Venus alone in the night sky.
I gravitate toward the source, afraid to put my eye close
for fear of what might be lurking outside the door.

In the bedroom, my body is cold under heavy blankets.
I sit next to myself, oddly unable to mourn, my mortal
tether slipping away and so I rise and float, bump
against the ceiling and walls as I become one with the air.

The alarm clock sounds and music plays.
I skim over the floor, dart from window to door,
singing along to Marianne Faithfull—
We shall live again, shake out the ghost dance—
practicing to become something that goes
bump in the night.

WHAT I'M WEARING

Stranger's voice, over-aspirated, gurgling with desire
wafts through the air, shimmers in humidity, catches in my ear,
makes me second-guess the t-shirt, jeans and sandals.

What are you wearing?

Restlessness like a bad suit, if you want to know,
pockets filled with old boarding passes, luggage tags on my toes.
Memory and need bouncing like a cheap rubber ball,
floor to ceiling, wall to wall, that dull thud,
in some tireless kid's hand—harder, higher, faster.

What are you wearing?

Fear of the unknown like new Ray-Bans, super-stylin',
this tape will self-destruct in five-second dreams
running on a loop in my complacent, desk jockey mind.
I can say *yes* in twenty languages and speak none of them,
I've got a German friend who scolds me for never visiting Berlin,
ja, I say, *ja, ja, ja, ja* until I sound like a flooded engine.

What are you wearing?

I'm casting off responsibilities and people like a warm coat,
so this must mean something, this discarding.
I've got a fire sale cooking in my head, sticking my fingers
in and out of the flame until they blister, until the feeling comes back.
Who else, what else, must go until I'm naked,

so when you ask the question again I'll be unburdened, invisible, dematerializing into dust that catches the first strong wind blowing east out over the water to elsewhere.

THINGS TO DO IN DENVER WHEN YOU'D RATHER BE DEAD

check into a cheap room near the airport
on a dusty freeway frontage road

gorge on delivered pizza, throw it up
sit cross-legged and meditate
in the middle of a king-size bed

wait for his call

itemize the cost of this trip you can't afford
consider leaving early

acknowledge that flying 1,404 miles
to meet a stranger who has charmed you
on a sex app is unquestionably stupid

wait for his call

the leavening of despair to anger, search for solace
in the arms of another on the sex app

irrationally feel guilty, resist the urge to watch porn
binge two hours of Kardashians, return to despair
eat the leftover pizza crust

wait for his call

stare out the window into dark Colorado night
the lights of Denver pale against the sky

consider drowning in the indoor pool
pockets weighted with cell phone
books no one bought, incomplete poems

the next morning, when he knocks on the door
excuse at the ready, be already gone

don't wait for my call

ANOTHER MONICA BELLUCCI DREAM
– *after Twin Peaks; for all the Davids*

Last night, I had another Monica Bellucci dream.
I was in London writing a book. Monica called
and asked me to meet her at the White Horse pub.
She said she needed to talk to me.

When we met at the pub, David was there
but I couldn't see his face.

Monica was very pleasant. She had come alone.
We both had wine.

And then she said: *We're not going to talk about Paris.*
That moment has come and gone;
it is an answer with no question.

A very powerful, uneasy feeling came over me.
Monica looked out the window and indicated to me
that something was happening there. I turned and looked.
I saw myself. I saw myself from long ago
standing with David outside Covent Garden tube station.
The first time I ever came to London.

David holds me tightly and then he kisses me,
something he had never done before in public.
He says we are living inside a dream—
that we have become doppelgängers, tulpas.

We will return to the states as different people,
call each other by different names.

Nothing is the same after this.

I feel a pervasive melancholy, not only for things lost,
but of things to come that will also be lost.
I imagine my insides—intestines and stomach—cleaned out,
smooth and gleaming like new pipes
or the tub of a washing machine.
I scrub my flesh until I am a pale version of my former self.
A vestige. A cheap copy.

I go to bed hungry, chewing the inside of my cheek
until I taste blood.
My teeth are a puzzle in my mouth.

I am unrecognizable to myself.

Monica is ready to leave. She kisses me on both cheeks.
Then she asks a strange question: *Is it future or is it past?*
Now this is really something interesting to think about.
And then she says:
Oh, mio caro amico, there is fire where you're going.

THE UNREQUITED ARSONIST

It's not the love itself that burns, but the hunt.
From coast to coast, tire scorch and gasoline
in my wake or chemtrails for the flyover states.
Watch and wonder where I'll come down hard,
wheels sparking tarmac, raising alarms.
I made up my mind—and yours—
left nothing for the return trip.
It was a yes or no question that set me off,
your hemming and hawing
over our future an accelerant.
This is the mystery of combustion
you will solve too late.
I'm already in your city, your street, your bed
with my hair of embers on your pillow.

PART TWO
THIS IS NOT AMERICA

INCANTATION

Take airport parking slip,
mix with boarding pass,
sprinkle with train ticket
add hotel room key,
stir in phone messages,
simmer with postcards.
Hold scrap talismans close
and inhale deeply.
Now say, "London."
Repeat until ephemera reshapes,
turns into a paper airplane
big enough to lift you
over the sea.

IN TAVISTOCK SQUARE
– after Mrs. Dalloway

I am sleeping in the corner of your ghost house, Virginia,
your Blitz-bombed house now a hotel full of rooms,
not of one's own, but for a parade of neverending strangers.

I rub my hand over your hard, slick head in the square
wet with summer rain, your hawkish nose turned toward
the other bombsite, the metal bus a twisted bloom of blood.

Dickens wrote *Hard Times* on the other side of the trees
and I find that living here is hard and there is no time
for idealistic, broke dreamers. He wrote *Bleak House* there, too.

I am stubborn, Virginia. I come back again and again
even as this city pulls me close and pushes me away,
in love with bellow and uproar; London; this moment of June.

Perhaps I should reconsider the scattering of my ashes,
commit them to the breeze that blows through Bloomsbury.
Make me fertilizer; plaster; eye grit; nowhere; everywhere.

ROOM 335, ROYAL NATIONAL HOTEL

Black man from White City
bigger than a single bed
sucking on my titty
doesn't want to give me head

Heavy eyes and silence
there's no stiffness in his cock
seems to want compliance
he never took off his socks

No one will be coming
we are beyond limp and sore
for him this was slumming
I was cheaper than a whore

I thrive on the unknown
foreign hotels and danger
delete you from my phone
aborted sex with strangers

ROCHESTER STATION

Last leaves rustle against blue November sky,
and I am in front of Rochester Station,
the clickity-clack of the London train disappearing,
depositing me in dreamland,
and the tears come so unexpectedly that I choke,
turn my face to the whitewashed stone,
pray for inheritance or lottery, anything
to make this permanent.

An old woman shuffles past me,
hunched over, headed into the station,
then two boys, one on crutches, are running
for the next train.
They overtake the woman, pushing past,
and the hobbled one falls on the stairs,
his painful cry of *fuck* echoes out the blue door,
and the old woman smiles.

This little microcosm—before Peter arrives
to whisk me away to the sweet keep and Krys—
is the life I want to lead: the half-grey days,
those almost bare trees, the sound of trains,
the long electronic sigh of their departures
and arrivals.

DUKKER

The old woman blindsides me in Leicester Square,
pushes the scrub of flowers into my fingers,
the tinfoil holding the stems damp from her grip.

Take them, sweetheart. How about a pound?

She is Romani, her head in a scarf, her face a relief map
of all the places she has been driven from over the centuries.
Her voice an amalgamation of those same lands,
touched with a dash of cockney.

I want to hand them back, refuse the offering, go on my way
to wherever my way might be, but the woman seizes my hand,
holds it fast as our eyes meet. Her face goes slack with pity.

You have to get away from him, sweetheart.

I drop the coin on the pavement and run,
push past tourists and buskers in Piccadilly Circus.
Slumped on the steps of Eros, I open my fist
to see the flowers—weeds really—staining my skin,
filling the lines of my sweaty palm.
And here is another map: of who I was, who I will be,
where I'm going.

IN THE CUT

I remember you folded in half,
only your right side visible
in the kitchen doorway,
just enough to see your hand
on his hip, his arm
around your neck,
the passion in one eye.

I remember footsteps, yours and his,
on the steps, displacing air,
making me catch my breath,
causing twitters and whispers
from guests downstairs.

The night before, we walked
through wet London streets,
kissed at my door, your hands
on my hips, my arms around your neck,
passion in both eyes.

I forfeited my right to disappointment
when I put you back on the street,
watched 3 a.m. dark swallow you up.
Your interest no match for my self-sabotage.

When your note arrives two days later,
chiding me for not saying goodbye,
an ocean divides us.

I realize I should have unfolded you,
to read the whole message,
risked being cut in half.

NOSTALGIA

I always loved you best at a distance
voice a faint radio signal
an image lost in television snow

The idea of you
perfect and acquiescing
sculpted blonde and grinning

Then you momentarily resurface
tangible flabby and older
one wrong word and then another

Now you live in another time zone
always behind me
stay in the west

THE COMEDOWN

Wind turns my umbrella inside out
leaves me drenched in Piccadilly Circus

Buses break down, divert routes
leave me stranded on strange corners

Here's real London life instead of surface
where day to day living is full of borders

Where money flows without recourse
this city is no longer made for paupers

The comedown a strange recurrence
my expat dreams seem like madness.

VICTORIA GATE

Maybe she was crying before she got on the coach at Marble Arch, settled in the seat across from me, but by the time we reach Victoria Gate, tears stream down her face, mouth open to receive her own sacrament.

Indian, ageless in tasteful floral, a blue sweater despite summer heat, an iPod clutched in her hand. Traditional music bleeds from earbuds, then shifts to Bollywood techno beat. And still she cries. Along Bayswater Road, her glassy eyes reverential, meeting her gaze feels like blasphemy. Who is she missing or mourning, or maybe it's what—her own bed, mother's cooking, stillness.

London is short on sympathy when it comes to heartbreak and homesickness, not so subtly tells you to walk it off. But sometimes at night, when you're riding past Hyde Park and dusky silhouettes arm-in-arm are framed by bus windows, a familiar song can collapse resolve, make you reach for the red hammer over your seat to crack the escape glass. Then unbuckle and rise through the treetops until the lamp at Victoria Gate is a pinprick, insignificant, up to the stratosphere where equilibrium inverts and tears become the stars that will guide you home.

ATONEMENT

I am sitting in a London cinema watching Vanessa Redgrave make amends for a life of deceit, to a soundtrack of rushing water I believe subliminal, to drive home melancholy, but when silhouetted heads turn in search, I realize it is real. It is raining hard outside, echoing behind the screen, and suddenly your death comes rushing back to me, Christopher, whom I have not mourned.

Fifteen years ago we watched Vanessa give away Howards End, thrilled at elegant despair and handwringing, the way the rain never looked ugly there, was always just enough and never too much. When our sweaty young palms found each other's in the dark, our dreams came in fast whispers, the promise that we would go to London one day.

I am here now, Christopher, and I feel you near. I am writing these words for you in Leicester Square, the English rain cold and perfect on my skin, yet the ink does not smear. You will not let me forget so easily, although I have tried to make you a stranger, a casualty of your own vices.

My fear is that I passed you on the street, when you were homeless and addicted, unrecognizable ghetto scarecrow, invisible and all the same, part of the city landscape. Maybe you were behind the gas station in a cold sweat, shooting meth to forget the HIV shame. Swallowed up in pride.

Your death is a voicemail, left by another with a phone number. The somber tone is unmistakable, a hush earmarked for the dead.

Four days gone—long enough to have shaken off flesh gravity—I expect your ghost to rattle the unearthly chains of your discontent. Even when I skip the memorial, numb on the couch as twilight approaches, picking the memory of you like a scab, I realize that you are not so much a wound, but a scar that will never fade.

But today, you come back as the sound of rain and fill me up like a bucket until I brim. Not a dry eye in the house, anyway. So clever, you, subtle and un-paranormal. I mourn you with celluloid, Christopher, in dark rooms where stories unfurl, with rushing water, with a city that pulls me near and pushes me away, with clocks that always know the score.

THE VOYAGE IN
—January 20, 2006

A whale has lost its way on the Thames,
swimming up into the city, threatening to beach,
bringing crowds to every bank and bridge.
Delight turns to dismay as it bumps along,
bleeding out, disoriented in shallow water.
It chose a path out of cold salt sea
into a curving river re-carved by humans.
Seven tonnes of leviathan exposed
to elements beyond its control.
Helicopters fly, the news gives it a nickname,
and on a pontoon boat—a mercy mission—
it spasms and spouts once, a last salute.

Maybe this whale was here before, in 1913,
the year Virginia Woolf overdosed on Veronal,
long before she found rocks to line her pockets.
Did she read about it in the papers, find herself
humming in sympathy to its plight, envision
for the first time how current could be deliverance?
If she were a whale, they could not stop her,
and maybe in those last breaths the secret
of why a previous life is never truly erased,
with its unexplained longings and déjà vu,
would at last come into sharp focus.

That night, I dream I am churning upriver,
out of the estuary and past the barrier.

The lights of the city slipping focus
as I head to my beaching, my resting place.
Underneath its arches, these last words:
London Bridge.
All I'll ever need, a marker to homeground
etched above the waterline.

THE TURF

Under the Bridge of Sighs, down Hell's Passage,
it already sounds like a fairy tale,
but soon I'm sitting at a table, a half pint of bitter
in hand under a golden Oxford sky, and I am inhaling
big lung bucketsful of summer twilight air.

I left on the Fourth of July, my middle finger
to the colonies as I returned to the Motherland,
tread the familiar airport floors, dozed on the coach,
fell across an unfamiliar bed, yet feeling un-arrived,
un-wowed, un-spectacularized.

Until I am sitting with an Englishman and his wife,
my friends, at The Turf, this tiny pub
hidden behind ancient walls, where scholars
and comet-spotters drank themselves to genius,
where our former president smoked pot.
Only then do I feel that spark, when jetlagged
queasy stomach unclenches and this country
embraces me again, and I exhale deeply.

ENGLISH PASTORAL

Oxford summer
the cottage doors

open to the garden
where wood pigeons coo

& distant laughter drifts
over the stone wall

I sit at the end of a long table
paper rustling in the zephyr

watch a butterfly flutter in
float over the forget-me-nots

time stops freeze idyllic
electric blue sky tufted

with motionless cotton wool
the city in my head goes mute

as I succumb to countryside
content with birds & breeze

RITUAL
– for AO

Jesus taps me lightly on the back,
pokes my neck, catches in my hair.
Sometimes he slides down my cheek,
threatens to put out an eye,
hangs suspended on his cross over my lips.
Sometimes I catch his toes with my teeth,
or open my mouth wide and take him whole,
a sacrament, the cold metal sweet with sweat
where it has lain on your chest all day.
Sometimes Jesus just watches me
from a distance, a tiny shadow
at the center of your bare back as you sit
on the edge of my bed ready to leave.
And sometimes, when Jesus disappears
over your shoulder as you pull on your shirt,
I confess that I want you to stay.
As night turns into morning,
glorious to luminous,
come back to bed and let's go through
the mysteries of the cross once more.

IN THE AFTERLIFE MY FATHER IS A LONDON CAB DRIVER

The hotel concierge gestures toward the waiting taxi, its back door already open. I slide in, say good morning, and an American voice speaks back. Unmistakably my father, dead three days, smiling at me in the rearview mirror as he pulls into traffic on Bayswater Road. There's no destination, so we'll make a loop around Hyde Park, long enough for him to tell me to be happy, healthy and wise—to not give up on the dream of really being here when I wake. Leave it to Daddy-O to leave it this way, to meet me on beloved ground he'd only heard about from my stories or watched on TV. When I think of my father now, he will always be in London, not gasping like a fish in a hospital bed as his heart went still. His new chosen profession to ferry the living between the stations of their grief, jovially tipping his cap as he drops fares at the corner of the rest of their lives.

MIDNIGHT IN A PERFECT WORLD
– Russell Square, London

Standing in line at Tesco,
clutching milk and batteries,
my American life drops away.
I blend, become unrecognizable
even to my reflection staring back
in the frozen foods door.
My needled skin like sleeping limbs
as if this perfect night is a dream
from which I never want to wake.

ACKNOWLEDGMENTS

Atticus Review: "I Should Be So Lucky," "In the cut" and "Killing Time"

Blue Fifth Review: "Another Monica Bellucci Dream"

Contemporary American Voices: "20th Century Boy"

The Cortland Review: "The unrequited arsonist"

Diode: "Ritual"

diversecity: "What I'm Wearing"

Flycatcher: "In Tavistock Square"

Foglifter: "In the afterlife my father is a London cab driver"

Homeground: "Rochester Station"

Impossible Archetype: "Strange Weather"

Luna Luna: "Nineteen" and "Nostalgia"

New Trespass: "Ghost Dancing"

Reading Queer: Poetry in a Time of Chaos: "Revenant"

This assignment is so gay: LGBTIQ Poets on the Art of Teaching: "Night Ride Home"

VerseWrights: "Atonement," "Incantation" and "Victoria Gate"

Many thanks and much love to Karen Head, Julie E. Bloemeke, Cecilia Woloch, Steven Reigns, Ivy Alvarez and A. VanSickle for their invaluable thoughts and suggestions on these poems. And to Bryan Borland, Seth Pennington and Sibling Rivalry Press for making me part of this wondrous family of writers.

ABOUT THE AUTHOR

Collin Kelley is the author of the American Library Association-honored poetry collection *Render* (Sibling Rivalry Press), as well as *Better To Travel* (Poetry Atlanta Press) and a chapbook, *Slow To Burn* (Seven Kitchens Press). Sibling Rivalry Press is also the publisher of his acclaimed *Venus Trilogy* of novels, *Conquering Venus*, *Remain In Light*, and *Leaving Paris*. A recipient of the Georgia Author of the Year Award and Deep South Festival of Writers Award, Kelley's poetry, reviews, essays and interviews have appeared in magazines, journals and anthologies around the world. For more, visit www.collinkelley.com.

ABOUT THE PRESS

Sibling Rivalry Press is an independent press based in Little Rock, Arkansas. It is a sponsored project of Fractured Atlas, a nonprofit arts service organization. Contributions to support the operations of Sibling Rivalry Press are tax-deductible to the extent permitted by law, and your donations will directly assist in the publication of work that disturbs and enraptures. To contribute to the publication of more books like this one, please visit our website and click *donate*.

Sibling Rivalry Press gratefully acknowledges the following donors, without whom this book would not be possible:

Liz Ahl	Bill La Civita
Stephanie Anderson	Mollie Lacy
Priscilla Atkins	Anthony Lioi
John Bateman	Catherine Lundoff
Sally Bellerose & Cynthia Suopis	Adrian M.
Jen Benka	Ed Madden
Dustin Brookshire	Open Mouth Reading Series
Sarah Browning	Red Hen Press
Russell Bunge	Steven Reigns
Michelle Castleberry	Paul Romero
Don Cellini	Erik Schuckers
Philip F. Clark	Alana Smoot
Risa Denenberg	Stillhouse Press
Alex Gildzen	KMA Sullivan
J. Andrew Goodman	Billie Swift
Sara Gregory	Tony Taylor
Karen Hayes	Hugh Tipping
Wayne B. Johnson & Marcos L. Martínez	Eric Tran
Jessica Manack	Ursus Americanus Press
Alicia Mountain	Julie Marie Wade
Rob Jacques	Ray Warman & Dan Kiser
Nahal Suzanne Jamir	Anonymous (14)

www.ingramcontent.com/pod-product-compliance
Lightning Source LLC
Chambersburg PA
CBHW021000090426
42736CB00010B/1396